행시야
놀자
11

INTERESTING

✔ 지혜로운 여러분의 도전을 기다리는 行詩
✔ 아직까지 경쟁자가 없었던 독보적인 作品

쉬운영어행시
EASY ENGLISH

정 동 희 저

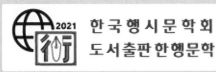

2021 한국행시문학회
도서출판 한행문학

128 쪽
160 편
수록

미친 저자 – 영어 전공자 아님 / 미국 유학파 아님 / 올해 나이 70세

쉬운영어행시
EASY ENGLISH

행시야 놀자 시리즈 #11집을 내면서

Every line poem bilingual	영 한 행 시
Almost poor articles but	어 설 퍼 도
Short sentence I'd write	단 출 하 고
You can see simple style	어 감 좋 다
Especial acrostic poetry	정 통 행 시
Now motive is caused	동 기 유 발
Great strange writings	희 한 한 글
Let it be only and unique	유 일 무 이
It's the first of Korea	한 국 최 초
See English-Korean translation	영 한 대 역
However study language	어 학 공 부

2021년 4월

한국행시문학회장 六峰 정 동 희

preface

Easy English Line Poem "쉬운영어행시" 차례

시조 행시(18)   SI JO line poem   PP 8~17
Abc 미사일, **Ace** 삼행시 / **Age** 나 지금, **Alc** 한잔 술 / **Cow** 소 죽통, 희망가 / **Die** 사고사, 코사지 / **Hee** 잘 큰 몸, 정동희 / **Hit** 가만히, **Hot** 신세계 / **JPN** 일 본 놈 / **May** 멋진 방 / **Sea** 동해항, 팽목항 / **Soy** 수채화 / **Win** 삼행시

3 행시(42)   3 line poem   PP 18~37
ABC 중국몽 / **Ago** 어고우, 지금이 / **All** 다 모여 / **Bud** 개화기, 꽃다발, 작약꽃 / **But** 그러나, 아니면, 하지만 **Cow** 소 죽통 / **DNA** 성탄절 / **Eel** 뱀장어 / **God** 이 밤도, 지도인, 하나님, 헤세드 / **GPS** 내 위치, 하나님 / **Joy** 단 석 줄 좋아요 / **JPN** 반도체, 안 산다 / **May** 나누기 / **Sea** 갈매기, 세월호, 조각배, 조바심 / **Soy** 콩나물 / **Top** 삼행시 / **Try** 트라이, 트라이, 해볼까 / **Wit** 사랑해, 위하삼, 정동길, 주먹시 / **WWW** 주주주 / **you** 당나귀, 당신은, 사랑해, 삼행시

4 행시(16)   4 line poem   PP 38~47
Beer 맥주 한잔 / **Best** 미친 저자 / **Life** 가시나요, 안고 가자 **Lord** 삼위일체, 주일성수 / **Love** 해바라기 **Soul** 해바라기 **Mark** 마가복음 / **SIJO** 시조행시 / **Your** 네탓 내덕, 영어단어 **What** 내로남불, 내로남불 / **It is** 시험 지속, **Soon** 한번 해봐

contents

5 행시(14)　　5 line poem　　　　PP 48~57

Bible 성경 한 귀절 / **Crazy** 영미에 올인 / **Dokdo** 민감한 그곳 / **Dream** 좋은 날 오길 / **Jesus** 주님께 영광 **Me too** 나도 피해자, 나도 피해자 / **North** 세기의 만남, 남쪽 대통령 / **Three** 군번이 세 개 / **Virus** 데칼코마니, 아주 위험해 / **World** 빛나는 세상 / **Yours** 당신의 것

6 행시(11)　　6 line poem　　　　PP 58~67

Almost 한국행시문학 / **Corona** 잠시 멈춤 동선 **Lovely** 미운 정 고운 정 / **Mother** 어머니의 기도, 부모에게 효도 / **Seraph** 차 한잔의 여유 / **So easy** 쉬운 영어 행시 / **Stroke** 웃어 두 혀 알지 / **Sunset** 노을 빛 하늘가 **Puzzle** 퍼즐 행시 쓰기 / **You win** 가진 건 없지만

7 행시(10)　　7 line poem　　　　PP 68~77

English 영어는 쉽지 않다 / **Friends** 친구는 나의 스승 **May it be** 반드시 이루소서 / **New year** 지금 햇살 밝구나 **No Japan** 사지도 가지도 마 / **October** 시월의 마지막밤 **Olympic** 방사능 경연대회 / **Profile** 내가 걸어온 흔적 **Scarlet** 아름다운 주먹시 / **You shut** 그 정도 하시지요

contents

8 행시(10) 8 line poem PP 78~87

Achilles 내게 제일 힘든 부분/**Calendar** 한행문학 새 카렌다
Deadline 더 있으면 다 망한다/**Gold moon** 달빛 젖은 금빛 물결
In autumn 9월 그도 도한 하늘/**Line poem** 천재거나 바보거나
Marlboro 하늘같은 내 여인아/**Lie House** 이 문제 결국 집이다
Waterloo 아바가 너무 좋아요/**Year is go** 새로운 미국 지도자

9 행시(8) 9 line poem PP 88~95

Available 평화통일과 한미동맹
Blueberry 블루베리 그대 내 사랑
Butterfly 오늘 나는 나비 한 마리
Hard to say 미안하단 말은 못해요
Mountains 가까운 산 그리고 인연
Myself all 나는 무엇으로 사는가
September 구월도 지나가는 달이다
Zacchaeus 잊혀진 그 설레임 잠시

10 행시(6) 10 line poem PP 96~101

Corona blue 코로나로 인한 불안 없다
Jesus Cross 주가 가신 길 십자가의 길
Stay with me 내 곁에만 머물러요 부디
Summer wine 그 해 여름 내내 찜찜했다

Three Seven 일이삼사오 육칠팔구십
While alive 강을 건너면 안 되는 이유

11 행시(6)   11 line poem   PP 102~107

Astrazeneka 아스트라제네카 맞아볼까
Corona Virus 좀 나댕기지 마 고집 접어요
Interesting 그것에 관심 있어?(ㄱㄱㄱㄱㄱㄱㄱㄱㄱㄱ)
It was Friday 일단 짤막한 행시가 좋아요
Times a while 소중한 시간 속 소중한 약속
Today's pains 오늘 고통은 내일의 향기다

12 행시(4)   12 line poem   PP 108~111

Abcdefghijkl 참 좋은 나의 벗 그 이름은 행시
Autumn leaves 내 인생 가을에 단풍잎 붉을까
Winter season 눈꽃이 보고파 겨울 비 내리고
Winter season 올 겨울 맞아서 일 한번 내볼까

13 행시(4)   13 line poem   PP 112~115

Because of fall 가을이 고독하게 만든 때문일까
I need you Jesus 오 전능하신 하나님 나의 예수님

contents

Green color you 겨울의 길목 딛고 넘어서 다시 봄
October Forest 낙엽이 더욱 고운 나의 가을 동화

14 행시(4)   14 line poem   PP 116~119

Ghijklmnopqrst 가나다라마바사아자차카타파하
Don't forget poem 가나다라마바사아자차카타파하
Korean language 한글날 우리 글 행시인은 행복하다
Pretty blue eyes 그대 맑은 눈동자에 나 자신이 잠겨든다

15 행시(2)   15 line poem   PP 120~121

English Line Poem 영어로 쓰는 행시 한글로도 멋진 행시
Love your destiny 네 운명을 사랑하라 니체가 한 말이지

16 행시(2)   16 line poem   PP 122~123

National Cemetery 나는 누가 뭐라 해도 대한민국 공인이다
The end of the month 오늘은 5월의 끝날 조용히 마무리한다

17 행시(2)   17 line poem   PP 124~125

Abcdefghijklmnopq 태우지도 못할 지독한 가슴은 이제 묻어라
The world is not easy 세상은 절대로 만만하지 않아요 해보세요

contents

Sijo Line Poem
시조 행시

Abc 에이 비 시

America pushing the bluff and UN give them too
By with missile firing again at Musudanri n-Korea
Continuously didn't care about Japanese threaten

미국은 엄포 놓고 유엔은 겁 주는데   **착착 준비 중**
사고 칠 무수단리 새 준비 마친 북한
일본이 쌍심지 켜도 눈도 꿈쩍 안 하네

Ace 에이스, 고수

Always myself is here within 3 line poems
Continued sentences with go and stop
Every time poet is green in poetic rhyme

三행의 문장 안에   삼삼한 내가있다   **삼행시**
行함과 멈춤들이   행렬로 이어지고
詩심과 운율속에서 시인은 늘 푸르다

Age 나이

Am I foolish poet just grow older?
Generally I used to have all night and now too
Even today also I forgot to sleep on line poems

나는야 나만 먹은 철없는 詩人인가　　　　　**철없는 詩人**
지난 밤 꼴딱 새고 지금도 뜬눈인데
금일도 行詩 속에서 잠들 생각 잊었다

Alc 알코올(=alcohol)

Alive today in my once of life
Let's think the right without tricks
Could have block is solved and stress out

한번인 내 삶에서 오늘을 살고 있다　　　　　**한잔 술**
잔 머리 접어 두고 순리로 생각하자
술 술 술 잘만 풀리고 스트레스 날린다

Cow 소

Coming rumors but no vaccine yet
Often full care and even if unlucky
Without pain maybe sick and die

소문만 무성하고 백신은 요원한데　　　　　　**소띠해**
죽어라 조심해도 재수에 옴 붙으면
통증도 느끼기 전에 확진 되고 죽을라

Cow year opening with a hope
Only can't see the way to fill hole
Whatever reduced outing just for me

희소식 기대하며 새해를 열고 있다　　　　　　**희망가**
망실감 채워 줄 길 아직은 안 보이고
가급적 나들이 줄여 내 한 몸만 챙긴다

Die 죽다, 사망하다, 돌아가다, 사라지다

Dead man has left then easy forget but
In oddly the nasty rumors don't stop till now
Every day I'd like ask the fact but impossible

사람이 없어지면 쉬 잊게 마련인데   **죽어도 산 듯**
고약한 소문 꼬리 그치질 않는구나
사실을 묻고 싶지만 그도 저도 못하네

Do not get lucky, you can have corona
I don't know fate tomorrow so look at all sides
Even if you are bored you'd better stay at home

코 꿰면 재수 없이   코로나 걸릴까 봐   **코로나**
사람 일은 모르니   사방을 살펴 본다
지금은 집콕 하면서 지겨워도 참아라

Hee 정동HEE

He is not handsome but nice guy
Even if not much help however constant
Even though lightweight but button up

잘 난 놈 아니지만 그래도 밉진 않다   **자화상**
큰 보탬 못 되지만 언제나 변함 없다
몸집은 크지 않지만 입 하나는 무겁다

Honesty and healthy is my everything
Equipment for long way when morning dawns
Energetic flying to hopeful next generation

정직과 성실함과 건강이 나의 전부   **정동희**
동녘이 밝아오면 먼 길 갈 채비하고
희망의 다음 세대로 힘껏 날아 오른다

Hit 타격, 적중, 성공, 안타, 히트작품

However a drizzle come down small branch
I touch and trim good writing on later life
Today it grin those to be hit hidden work

가녀린   가지 끝에   가랑비   내려앉고
만년에   만개한 글   만지고   다듬는데
히트할   히든 작품이   히죽히죽   웃는다

출품 준비

Hot 뜨거운

Hungry on now severe crisis
On corona situation I may die
The hot potato in the cold wave

송년을 보내면서 주린 배 움켜쥔다
죽을지 살지 모를 코로나 심각한데
매서운 한파 속에서 북한 원전 뜨겁다

송구영신

JPN = Just Punitive Nation 천벌 받을 나라

Just called good job man after finished job
Put your interest down about my daily life
Never eat Dokdo-shrimp even if they born again

일 보고 돌아서면 일 본 놈 되는 거야   **일 본 놈**
본관이 누굴 만나 뭘 먹든 상관 말어
놈들은 죽었다 깨도 독도새우 못 먹어

May   ~할 것이다, ~할 수도 있다

My dreamlike space with full of nice writings
All the time put in true heart and hot desire
You every visit here I'll welcome with a smile

멋진 글 가득 열린 꿈 같은 나의 공간   **멋진 방**
진정한 마음 담고 뜨거운 열망 실어
방문객 오실 때마다 방긋방긋 웃으리

Sea 바다

Still my mind toward east and east only
Everyday want to see sunrise at the water surface
Also want to see a cute seagull fly around the port

동으로 동으로만 마음이 달려간다   **동해항**
해수면 솟구치는 붉은 해 보고 싶고
항구에 곱게 날아들 갈매기도 보련다

Spurt sun is hot within tight tensions
Even body buried at sea but soul had gone
A quiet requiem with silence hung over the port

팽팽한 긴장 속에 솟는 해 뜨겁지만   **팽목항**
목표는 수장되고 영혼은 실종 상태
항구에 흐르는 정적 소리 없는 진혼곡

Soy 콩

Sometimes run there hundred miles away
Open the chat window in the vegetable field
You know store my phone lovely image of you

일상

수백 리 먼 길에도　수시로 달려간다
채마 밭 메다가도　채팅창 열어보고
화사한 그대 영상을　화면 속에 심는다

Win 승리하다, 우승하다, 이기다, 따다

What a beautiful steps nice 3-4-3-4

It's rhyme between sentences 3-5-4-3

Nowadays time passes remain trend of the world

삼행시

삼삼한 발걸음에   **삼**빡한 삼사삼사

행간에 운 넣은 글   **행**마는 삼오사삼

시간이 이리 흘러도 **시**류만은 여전해

3 Line Poem
3 행시

ABC Anything But China(중국만 빼고)

Anything but China
By the strengthen international cooperation
Cut off the whole relationship

- 미국은 다르다 -

중국만 빼고
국제 공조 강화로
몽땅 끊는다

시진핑의 연내 방한에 매달리고 있는 한국의 '중국몽'과는 달리
미국이 중국을 대하는 태도는
"**ABC(=Anything But China** : 중국만 빼고) 방침"이며
아래와 같은 멘트로 중국에 대한 압박성 경고를 날리고 있습니다
"**We could cut off the whole relationship**"
"**중국과 모든 관계를 끊을 수도 있다**"라고..

Ago 지난, 이전에

After all go away

Go out of sight the worry

Only stand it

어차피 간다

고민도 사라진다

우선 참아라

At this time

Go away just quickly

Only past time

지금 이 시간

금방 사라집니다

이미 옛 시간

All 모두, 다, 전부

Anybody come on challenge it　　다들 와서 도전해
Let's try it all line poem anyway　　모두 행시가 되는
Let's make it English and Korean　　여기 영한 대역시

* 대한민국에서 영어깨나 하시는 분들은 다 도전하세요..
영어로도 행시가 되면서..한글로도 행시가 되는 작품..
도전에 성공하시면 아래와 같은 특전을 드립니다..

1. 한국행시문학에 가입 후 매일 영어 행시 쓰기(무료)
2. 한국행시문학회 회원 대우(무료)
3. 일정 수준 도달시 시인 등단 기회(비용이 거의 없음)
4. 한국 문단에서 기성 문인으로 대우(바로 시행)
5. 최근 발간된 행시집 10권(10종) 증정(무료)
6. 본인 작품으로 시집 발간시 최저 염가로 편집 및 출판
7. 한국문인협회 회원 입회 자격 부여

* 상담전화 : 010-6309-2050　六峰 정동희 회장
* **30인 이상 단체 요청시 저자 출강(영어행시, 영어회화 노하우)**

Bud 봉오리, 싹

Blossoms forsythia 개나리 만발
Under the bright days of spring 화창한 봄 날씨에
Day by day mood of pleasure 기분이 쾌청

Bunch of flowers   꽃 다 발
Usually all flowers bloom 다 피 다
Dreamlike pretty bouquet 발 다 꽃

Beautiful one even small 작지만 예뻐
Under the trust promised 약속된 신뢰 속에
Day by day in full blossom 꽃망울 활짝

But 그러나, 아니면, 하지만

But when I go to the town   그 동네 갈 때
Usually I've been meet rush hour   러시 아워 만나고
Therefore I have a hard time   나도 힘들어

But I don't like you   아니꼽지만
Usually feel your poor life   니 인생 불쌍해서
Therefore give you a indulgence   면죄부 준다

But in less than a day   하루도 안 돼
Usually something be chastised   지탄 받을 일들이
That's happen every day   만날 생긴다

Cow 소, 암소

Choice always on eat less
Often even if eat just gruel
We live in communication

소식하면서
죽만 먹고 살아도
통하며 산다

DNA 디옥시리보 핵산(Deoxyribo-Nucleic Acid)

Do not angry   성 내지 마라

Never doing sigh   탄식도 하지 마라

Absolutely not good   절대 안 좋다

Eel 뱀장어

Eat a hot snake soup

Enhance the energy and guts

Lots of blood circulates well

뱀탕 먹으면

장도 정력도 튼튼

어혈도 풀려

God 신, 하나님

God is the master of this land   이땅의 주인
Only he made night and day   밤과 낮을 만드신
Day by day he give great love   도톰한 사랑

Good watch to be safe in God   지켜 주시고
Only help to be wise with you   도와 주시옵시고
Day by day guide well me please   인도 하소서

Great only you   하나 뿐인 님
Of course you will be keep me   나를 지켜 주실 님
Dreamlike you are Jehovah   님은 여호와

Great immeasurable love but   헤아릴 수 없지만
Only the value be countable   세어볼 만한 가치
Day by day we've Jesus love   드높은 주의 사랑

* 헤세드(hessed) : 하나님의 사랑, 긍휼, 자비

GPS 위성항법장치(Global Positioning System)

Great my line poem   내가 쓴 행시

Put together up and down   위 아래 손질한다

Soaring high happiness   치솟는 기쁨

God's will I know it   하나님 뜻을 아네

Power is thanks with God to me   나에게 감사는 힘

Success give us from the Lord   님이 주시는 형통

Joy 기쁨, 즐거움, 환희, 행복

Just 17 letters short sentence   단문 십칠 字

Only long time watch for chance   석 달 열흘 벼르며

You know it's the best poem   줄 세운 名詩

Join wonderful English poem   좋은 글 만나

Often be very happy   아주 행복해 하는

You know me like this?   요런 날 알까?

JPN 일본(Japan) - N● JPN -

Just overcome this situations   반드시 극복

Pushback to them as it is   도로 돌려 주면서

Now we change the system   체질 바꾼다

Just no driving those car   안 타 그런 차

Perhaps didn't buy them before   산 일도 없었지만

Never buy such things again   다시는 안 사

May ~것이다, ~할 수 있다, ~ 하기를

My short sentences	나의 짧은 글
Actually a tonic for somebody	누구에게는 보약
Your funnily line poem too	기묘한 행시

Sea 바다

So cool with a west wind — 갈바람 시원

Every time feels good when visit — 매번 바다가 좋아

A cup of soju give me nice mood — 기분에 한잔

Stop the passage of time — 세류 멈추고

Even moonlight has bluish — 월색은 창연해도

Alive breathing is tough — 호흡 거칠다

So small one — 조금은 작은

Even pointed edge and behind — 각진 모서리 뒤로

Abdomen fulled ship — 배만 나온 배

Silent wave — 조용한 파도

Even sea's keep quiet — 바다는 침묵해도

Alive heart is beating — 심장은 뛴다

Soy 콩, 간장

Something like a beans

Often you look at me ignore

You eat only just water

콩만한 것이

나를 우습게 보네

물만 먹는 게

Top 위, 최고의, 상위, 가장

Three or four line poems   삼행 사행시

Only happy and lucky sentence   행복과 행운의 글

Poem of poems, just a top   詩중에 제일

한국행시문학회
한국 행 시 문 학
다음 카페/행시 쓰고 시인 된다
가입 문의 010-6309-2050
2002 - 2021

Try 노력하다, 해보다, 시도하다

Till to open your mouse 트기까지는

Rather than learn latin language 라틴어 보다 쉬워

You need just two months 이 개월 걸려

There are open space 트인 공간에

Real nice lilac aroma's full 라일락 향기 가득

Yeah~ It feels like living 이래서 살 맛

Try first and then 해보고 나서

Resolve about pack up or not 보따리 싸든 말든

You must act surely 자신 있게 해

Wit 재치, 지혜, 지성

With a love
I like romantic mood
The line poem's bright

사랑과 함께
랑만적인 분위기
해맑은 행시

Wit and clean
It's only patent writings
Three line poems cheers~!!

위트와 깔끔
하나뿐인 특허품
삼행시 만세~!!

Wonderful late autumn
I'd look around with my friends
Till to the twilight

정겨운 만추
동무들과 걸었네
길 저물도록

Writings as small as a fist
Including the ink rather well
The poetic sentiment rises

주먹 만한 글
먹물깨나 먹은 듯
시심이 인다

If we live 우리가 산다면

We live for the Lord

We die for the Lord

We belong to the Lord

주 위해 살고

주를 위해 죽나니

주의 것이라

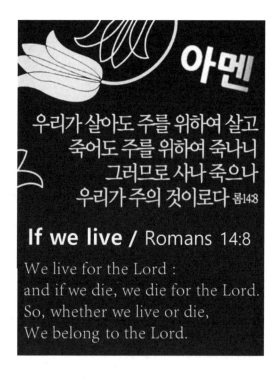

아멘

우리가 살아도 주를 위하여 살고
죽어도 주를 위하여 죽나니
그러므로 사나 죽으나
우리가 주의 것이로다 롬14:8

If we live / Romans 14:8

We live for the Lord :
and if we die, we die for the Lord.
So, whether we live or die,
We belong to the Lord.

You 여러분, 당신, 너, 자네

You're important but if not here
Only I'm useless person actually
Usually I have to go back heaven

당신 없으면
나는 쓸모도 없어
귀천해야 해

You are a sharp guy
Of course not a gentleman but
Usually I like you in my heart

당신 똑똑해
신사는 못 되지만
은근히 좋아

You know it's a real fact
Only I wanna date with you
Usually clear and bright you

사실 말인데
랑데부 하고 싶은
해맑은 그대

Your English poem is nice
Of course interline have straight
Usually so cool

삼삼합니다
행간이 반듯하고
시원합니다

Beer 맥주

Beer mixed <u>soju</u> become <u>somac</u>	맥주에 소주섞어 소**맥**
Even no snack brings binge drink	주안상 따로없어 폭**주**
Excess grudge in my blank heart	한구석 텅빈가슴 여**한**
Really delicate with beer bubble	잔잔한 거품속에 애**잔**

Best 최고의, 최선의

Be the American English accent   미국식 영어 발음
Each time speak with be familiar   친숙하게 구사해
Some people around the author   저자 주변 사람들
The maniac who admit by other   자타 공인 미친 놈

行詩 쓰는 詩人
육봉(六峰) 정동회
1951년생 010-6309-2050

미국식 영어발음 친숙하게 구사하는 美親저자 약력

한울문학 시 부문 등단
한국문인협회 회원
한국행시문학회 회장

도서출한 한행문학 대표
국내유일 행시문예지 **계간 한행문학** 창간·발행인

예비역 육군대령
영남대학교 4년/방송통신대학교 졸업
경기대 대학원 석사과정 수료
국군화생방방어연구소 방사능실장 역임(1피공득)
한미야전사령부 화생방...

Life 삶, 생명, 생활, 인생

Leave you here in a hurry   가시겠다니
It's bittersweet feeling anyway   시원 섭섭하네요
Finally I don't know my mind   나도 모르는 마음
Every day unknown world   요지경 세상

Let's carry with it   안고 갑시다
It hardship even though difficult   고난은 힘들어도
Financial problem is difficult   가난은 어려워도
Eventually those are my assets   자산이 된다

Lord 하나님(the Lord), 소유자, 군주(lord)

Look at revival in 3 days 　　　　삼일 만에 부활한
Only the one exist is 　　　　　위에 계신 단 한 분
Right here being trinity 　　　　일체로 오신 이 분
Dear my Lord without system 　　체제 초월 하나님

Lord, my God 　　　　　　　　주여 나의 하나님
On Sunday if go to church 　　　일요일 교회 가면
Really the holy spirit comes 　　성령이 임하시어
Day by day Lord blesses a lot 　수많은 복 주시네

Love 사랑하다, 좋아하다, 애정

Looking at until sunset   해질 때까지
Old love with heart   바랜 그리움 달고
Visit him as live   라이브로 오실 임
Everytime miss him also today   기리는 하루

Soul 영혼

Sometimes without the sun   해가 없어도
Only head full of desire   바라는 마음 가득
Usually heading for you in live 라이브로 향하는
Look tilted my soul   기운 내 영혼

Mark 마가(성경), 마크, 표시, 기록

Mind of rest   **마**음에 안식

Always warm words in mind   **가**슴 따스한 말씀

Really full of the good news   **복**된 소식 가득한

Keeping the voice   **음**성 지킨다

Sijo 시조(時調)

Sijo rhyme by designated form   시조 운율로
It has been in the gracefullness   조신하게 나선다
Join the rhyme with interline   행간에 운 붙이고
Open the poetic sentiment now   시심 펼친다

Your 당신의, 여러분의

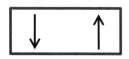

Your mistake is my fault   ↓네 잘못 내**탓**↑
Often thanks not only good luck   ↓덕 없음 감내↑
Usually thank you by your helping ↓내 호사 네덕↑
Right living without any complaint ↓**탓** 않고 사네↑

Your line poem bilingual   **영**한 대역 행시로
Only not a same word   **어**쨌던 중복 없고
Usually short sentences   **단**출한 짧은 문장
Really I'd write easily word sense **어**감상 쉽게 쓴다

What 무엇, 뭐라고?

When I do it even if illegal   내가 할 때는
However it's romance naturally   로맨스가 되지만
And if when others do it same   남이 그렇게 하면
That'll be scandal   불륜이 된다

When I buy that   내가 살 때는
However it's roman of course   로망이라 하지만
Another person buy that same   남이 사는 꼬라지
That'll be really inconvenient   불편해 못 봐

It is.. 그것은..

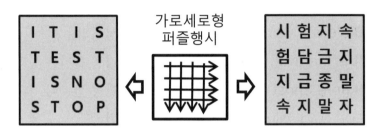

"**It is test is no stop**"
"시험이 멈추지 않는다"

Soon.. 곧..

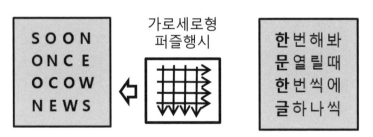

"**O**ne-**C**lick-**O**ne-**W**rite"
"한번 클릭할 때마다
한번 글 쓰기 운동"

Bible 성경

Bible is a word of the Lord   성스러운 말

It is the truth of the world   경종 울리는 진리

Before Christ to nowadays   한참 전부터

Live read valuable always   귀하게 늘 읽었던

Especially keep in my mind   절대 새길 말

Crazy 미치광이, 말도 안 되는, 괴짜, 훌륭한
- Crazy author introduction(美親 저자 소개)

Certainly I'm not English major   **영**어 전공자 아님

Really not studying in America   **미**국 유학파 아님

Actually full of energy   **에**너지가 넘치는

Zestful man on 70 years old now   **올**해 정열의 일흔

You know I'm a humanity guy   **인**간성 좋은 남자

Dokdo 독도

Dokdo shrimp and sciaenoid   민어와 독도새우

Octopus is attractive favor fish   감칠맛 나는 문어

Korean peninsula easternmost   한반도의 최동단

Dear picturesque treasure island   그림 같은 보물섬

Our ancestry soul in everywhere   곳곳에 조상님 얼

Dream 꿈

Dream a good dream	좋은 꿈 꾸고
Really expect big hit still	은근히 대박 기대
Especial date I bought it	날 잡아 샀다
Anyway 5,000 won lottery	오천 원어치 복권
May it be nice dream	길몽이 되길

Jesus 예수님

Jesus can solve that, trust in him   주님만 믿고

Even if it's difficult, rely to the him   님께 모두 맡기면

Surely he can get rid of mess   께름칙함도

Unbelievable it will be lost forever   영원히 없어지니

So it's a glory of God   광영이로다

Me too 나도 피해자, 나도 당했다

Me either I agree with you   나도 공감해
Even anybody never forgive that   도저히 용서 못해

To avoid damage is better   피해 없도록
Only share the right solutions   해법을 공유하고
Often notice again to others   자꾸 알리자

Maybe if our country is ruined   나라가 망한다면
Even though nowhere to escape   도망갈 곳도 없고

To be damaged only we have   피해 입을 수밖에
Only he laughts and deceives   해해 웃고 속이니
Only we are being fooled   자꾸 속을 수밖에

North 북, 북한(North Korea)

Now we have a hot issue   세 사람 모여
Observe about that more   기웃대며 살핀다
Really must not believe him   의심은 기본
The unification is earlier yet   만세는 이르지만
Honorable Korea is just one   남북은 하나

Nowadays feels disgraceful   남세스럽다
Only hateful bastard than Japan   쪽국보다도 밉고
Renovate Republic Of Korea   대한민국을
Total ruiner against proud Korea   통째로 말아먹은
However soulless guy   령혼 없는 자

"Jung, Dong-Hee" 六峰 정동희

There are 30 years for military
High rank full colonel as shiny
Right now I'm a line poems poet
Exactly I'm falling in 3 line poems
Especial way for pioneer

군대 삼십 년
번쩍이는 말똥 셋
이젠 행시인
세줄 시에 푹 빠진
개척자의 길

논산군번 12390274
하사군번 89002837
장교군번 257835

Corona Virus 코로나 바이러스

Valuable date booking from her   데이트 받고
I refused that just right away   칼같이 거절했다
Reason is afraid of corona virus   코로나 겁나
Usually can't go outside easily   마당도 못 나서니
So I needs something more   니즈만 는다

Very high risks so far   아직은 위기
It needed clean by myself   주변 청결 잘 하고
Risk places visiting and   위험 장소나
Usually avoid dangerous situation   험한 상황 피하고
So happy to you for a long time   해피하세요

World 세상

When I'm in light by line poem   빛을 받을 때
Only I'm alive as you know   나는 비로소 산다
Right now spending time slowly   는적대면서
Live in the world like this but   세상 살아가지만
Day by day always I'm happy   상시 즐겁다

Yours 당신의, 당신의 것

Yes I know that   물론 압니다
Of course I don't have to watch it   안 봐도 비디오라
Under the skies clear day clears   개인 하늘에
Raised up yours beauty   피어나는 그대의
So your nice smile   면 붉은 미소

6 Line Poem
6 행시

Almost 거의, 대부분

Anyway if we start it once   한번 시작한

Line poems with Korean-English   국문 영문 행시가

May it brings to us happy and   행복을 주고

Only give us full poetic sentiment 시심 넘치는

Sentence power also raise up so   문장력 키워주니

The best of learning effect it is   학습 효과 짱

* Daum 정통 행시 카페 : **한국행시문학** - 가입 환영

café.daum.net://3 Line Poem

2002년 10월 1일 개설, 현재 회원 수 1,300명

Corona 코로나19

Couldn't to sleep nowadays but   잠을 못 자도

Of course time goes by anyway   시간은 간다

Right now stopp the time   멈춘 건 세월이고

Only corona dances by themselves 춤추는 건 코로나

No moving forward line of flow   동선이 묶인

Actually too sadly in nice season 선한 계절아

Lovely 아름다운, 사랑스런, 예쁜

Let have foolish way	미련스럽게
Of course I think I'm lucky	운 좋다고 여기고
Vividly leave my mind to her	정을 맡긴다
Every day I feel a grateful	고마운 마음
Let's think I'm lucky	운 좋다고 생각해
You know give a good heart	정을 다 준다

Mother 어머니

Mother's words..   어머니 말씀..

Only go to church instead of money   머니 보다 교회다

Thou if don't know about that   니가 모르면

However you must not doubt it   의심하지 말아라

Every prayer has power and   기도의 힘은

Really it's endless actually   도무지 끝도 없다

Maybe every one knows that   부지 불식간

Only motherhood is great   모성은 위대

Theirs energy has full always   에너지 넘쳐나고

Her do not lazy as you know   게으르지도 않다

Especially the filial duty is basic   효행은 근본

Really we must do that well   도리는 마땅

Seraph 천사

So cold weather 　　　　　　　차가운 날씨

Even now with a cup of coffee 　한잔의 커피 속에

Rising old days calm memory 　잔잔한 추억

Almost meaningful to me 　　　의미가 있는

Perhaps go against many years 　여러 해를 거스른

Happy my childhood memories 　유년의 기억

So easy 아주 쉬워요

So easy it really   쉬워요 정말
Only with rhyme sentence   운 맞춘 단문

English-Korean bilingual   영어와 한글 대역
All writings are line poems   어법상 모두 행시
Some quick person have chance   행동 빠른 님
You'd better start right now   시작해 봐요

Stroke 뇌졸중, 발작, 타격 뇌졸중

Smile right now   웃어 보세요 지금

Talk any word   어떤 말을 하세요

Raise up two arms   두 팔을 들어 봐요

On hold forward your tongue   혀를 내밀어 봐요

Know this procedure   알아 두면

Even emergency!! it's very useful   지극히 유용해

* 뇌졸중을 영어로 STROKE라 하는데..
* S T R O K E 글자 중에서 처음 네 글자..
  즉, S T R O 를 알아두면 위험한 상황에서
  현장에서도 뇌졸중 초기증세를 확인할 수 있다
  우리말로는 '웃어두 혀'를 기억해 두고
  그 말의 뜻과 함께 알아두면..지극히 유용하다
  <웃어보라/어떤 말을 해보라/두 팔을 들어보라/혀를 내밀어라>

Sunset 노을, 일몰

Sunset become like yellow color   노랑 빛 노을

Under evening dark it have affair   을야와 야합하여

Now burning light to scarlet   빛을 태운다

Skies high at this season   하늘은 높고

Every time shows blue and then   늘상 푸른 빛이라

Too much flowed in my heart   가슴 벅차다

Puzzle 퍼즐

Puzzle type line poem is	퍼즐 행시란
Usually very fun for us	즐거운 존재
Zoom in and out with line poem	행시 속에서 줌을
Zeal through the poem	시를 통한 열정을
Listen and writes of them	쓰고 들으며
Erect my energetic spirit	기를 살린다

행시야놀자 시리즈 #9

퍼 즐 행 시 집
六峰 정 동 희

퍼 즐 행 시 집 나 왔 어 요
무 엇 이 **퍼** **즐** **행** **시** 인 지
이 런 **걸** 알 아 보 **시** 고 요
어 **떻** 게 답 인 지 몰 **라** 도
기 **어** 이 해 보 면 알 **고** 요
진 짜 로 어 렵 긴 **하** 지 요
해 보 면 다 아 **는** 거 지 만
절 대 로 쉽 **지** 않 은 거 라
어 떨 때 는 **쪽** 헤 매 다 가
잘 될 때 는 **요** 렇 게 돼 요
재 미 있 게 읽 어 보 세 요

한 국 행 시 문 학 회
도 서 출 판 한 행 문 학

You win 하면 된다, 네가 이긴다

Year by year, day by day 가면 갈수록

Outstanding line poems real fun 진짜 즐거운 행시

Usually nice healthy day 건전한 하루

Without good skills to write 없는 글 솜씨

I'm writing continued tireless 지치지 않고 쓰니

Now I'm satisfying more 만족도 커져

7 Line Poem
7 행시

English 영어

English is easy	영어는 쉽다
Naturally language is talking	어학은 말하는 것
Going even though you'd slowly	는적거려도
Lovely speaking is just simple	쉽게 말할 수 있다
I advice to you to do now	지금 해보라
Surely could back if you stop it	앓는다면 퇴보다
How about try it again	다시 해보라

국(極)서정시 주먹 行詩를 곁들인

영어 행시

단어 공부에 일조
영작 실력 저절로

Jung Dong-Hee

짧은 문장 위주로
영어 회화에 도움

도서출판 한행문학

nglish

* 행시야 놀자 시리즈 제7집 *

Friends 친구

Friends are my teachers   친구는 스승

Real bead is too clear for me   구슬처럼 맑아서

If I waste time for a while   는적거려도

Even though my lack is mirrored   나의 부족함 비쳐

Normally it with justice   의리와 함께

Day by day come friendly teacher   스승처럼 다가 와

So he help me to win   승리 도우네

May it be 되게 하소서

Maybe straight courage	**반**듯한 용기
Actually it with high will	**드**높은 기상으로
You know I've begun	**시**작했노라
It's clear bright path	**이** 길은 분명 밝은
The ruby color brilliance	**루**비 빛 광채
Brightly the path to wish	**소**망 빛내줄 그 길
Eventually I'm rushing	**서**둘러 간다

New year 새해

2 0 2 1

HAPPY NEW YEAR

NOW WE MEET AN ANOTHER DAWN
EVERYDAY WILL BE NOT JUST SAME
WONDERFUL SUNNY EAST WINDOW

YEAR BY YEAR WE EXPECT NEW DAY
EVERY THIS TIME WE PRAY THE SAME
ALWAYS WANT HEALTH AND UTOPIA
RED SUN MAY GIVE US THE ANSWER

지금 우리는 새 여명을 만난다
금일과 꼭 같지는 않을 것이나
햇살 머금은 멋진 동창을 보며
살가운 새 날을 우린 기다리고
밝은 이맘때 같은 기도를 하며
구리빛 건강 유토피아 빌지만
나의 답을 태양이 줄 수도 있다

No Japan 일본은 없다

Nobody buy them

Of course choice carefully now

Just it thief's things

Are you going to there why?

Perhaps not this time to visit

Anything about that understand?

Never buy and never go there

사는 일 없다

지금 잘 보고 사라

도둑놈 물건

가더라도 왜 거길?

지금은 아냐

도대체 이해가 돼?

마땅히 지켜

October 10월

On these days feeling unsatisfied　시답잖아서

Create reschedule for monthly　월간계획 또 짜고

Tie the strong will and then　의지를 담아

Only heading up toward last goal　마지막 골을 향해

Burn with fight continue　지속적으로

Energetic full power push them　막강하게 민다면

Really would be stop deep night　밤도 끝나리

Olympic 올림픽

Of course if you without carefully   **방**심한다면

Lots of radioactivity attact to you   **사**정 없이 맞는다

You must prevent by your ability   **능**력껏 막자

May you eat without any guard   **경**계 없이 먹으면

Perhaps even if very low level   **연**한 농도도

It is very dangerous and then   **대**단히 위험해서

Caution!! You can die suddenly   **회**까닥 사망

＊ 저자 방사능 분야 약력

¤ 예비역 육군 대령(화생방 장교)

¤ 국군화생방방어연구소 핵물리장교, 방사능실험실장 역임

¤ 한국원자력연구소 20주 연수 / 정문규 박사에게 사사

¤ 방사능동위원소(Radio Isotope) 취급면허획득

¤ 육군장교영어반 6개월 과정 수료

¤ 한미연합야전사 화생방보좌관 역임(의정부)

¤ 한미연합사령부 화생방과장 역임(용산)

Profile 프로필, 옆모습, 개요, 윤곽

Powerful 70 years old now   내 나이 칠십

Running live a long but thin life   가늘고 길게 산다

Only quicker than others   걸음 빠르고

First lead in most of them   어지간히 앞장 서

I'd like a stir all around   온 데 휘젓고

Left the trail here and there   흔적이 여기 저기

Everywhere looks pretty much   적잖게 보여

Scarlet 주홍색

So far we've long way to go but	아직 멀지만
Cute and more smart and	름름하고 근사한
Always nice letters and then	다부진 글에
Rhyme the line as pretty too	운까지 곱게 넣어
Light on others besides	주변 밝히고
Even open up in the chest also	먹먹함도 풀어 줄
Therefore I'll write the line poem	시를 쓰리라

You Shut 그 정도 하시지요

You shut mouse
Only politicians have been doing
Unbelievably too much full

그 입 닫아라
정치인들 하는 짓
도가 넘친다

Small minded like little working
However it is valueless then
Usually improper and ashamed
There is very strange

하는 일 좀스럽고
시시하더니
지금도 민망하고
요상하구나

Achilles 아킬레스(건)

As you know my big defect is	내 큰 결점은
Caused by habitual lazy	게으름 때문이다
However missed time and then	제 때를 놓쳐
It raised work to great height	일만 잔뜩 키우고
Lots of case be more powerful	힘은 더 드니
Leak point is unsure always	든든하지 못한 점
Every defect need to be changed	부족한 점은
So I have to change it actually	분명히 바꿔야 해

Calendar 카렌다, 달력

Creative Han-Haeng publishing 한행문학에
Artistic calendar has come out 행시 달력 나왔다
Literary nice works within there 문학 작품이
Especially brilliant beautiful day 학처럼 빛나는 날
New mind with our members 새로운 마인드로
Dreamlike calendar was born 카렌다 탄생
Actually creation not borrowed 렌트 아닌 창작품
Really great attempt for it 다양한 시도

Deadline 데드라인, 마감시한

Do you know what we've remain? 더 줄 게 있나?

Earlier our possess gave all them 있는 것 다 퍼줬고

Already be a big snarl to us 으름장이 심 해서

Day by day increased immunity 면역 생겼어

Looks like the next order will be 다음 순서는

It's only to be destroyed 망하는 것 뿐이야

No KOREA to us from now 한국은 이제 없어

Ending dinner we have only 다 끝난 거야

Gold Moon 골드 문

Go straight ahead	달려 나간다
Only fast speed like a light	빛과 같은 속도로
Less than get wet	젖지 않을 정도의
Dried rainy road	은은한 빗길
Man like precious	금쪽 같은 님
On the light my here comes	빛을 타고 오시니
Of course like fish with water	물 만난 고기처럼
Now it'll be good fruitful	결실 맺으리

In Autumn 가을에

In late september of someday   구월 하순 어느날

North over incident happened   월북 사건이 났다

                                                          그렇게 발표 됐다

Announced that by authorities

Unbelievable lawless persons did   도도한 사람들이

The firing provocatively   도발적 사격으로

Ultimately they killed a life   한 생명을 죽였다

Maybe the sky is indifferent   하늘도 무심하지

Now I always resent about that   늘 원망만 해본다

Line poem 행시行詩(acrostic)

Let see a thousand and more	**천** 번 만 번을
I measure again and again	**재** 보고 또 재어도
Now short and outspoken writing	**거**침없는 짧은 글
Every time I like it	**나**는 좋아요
Perhaps it's desirable writings	**바**람직한 글
Of course even push and push	**보**채고 또 보채도
Every time shows stable level	**거**의 일정한 수준
Most of all I love it	**나**는 좋아요

* acrostic : 각 행의 첫 글자 또는 마지막 글자를 맞추면
　　　　　　(세로로 읽으면) 하나의 말이 되는 시

Marlboro 말보로(담배 이름)

Man of one day means one year   하루가 일년

Always miss you actually   늘 보고 싶은 그대

Remember only just one woman   같은 여인 떠올려

Love as quiet anyway   은은한 사랑

Because of I like you   내가 좋아서

Of course I love you   사랑한 내 연인아

Romance is more needed to us   랑만도 못 나누고

Over went far away   아주 갔구나

MARLBORO =

Man **A**lways **R**emember **L**ove **B**ecause **O**f **R**omance **O**ver

"남자는 흘러간 로맨스 때문에 사랑을 기억한다"

* 이 글은 말보로 탄생 비화를 생각하면서 만든 작품입니다

* 인터넷 검색 ➜ 말보로 담배 이름 탄생의 비화

Previous Regime 역대 정권

LH, SH, BH of 'H' means 'house'
It's houses have lot of problems
Each houses with unlucky too

이 의미는 '집'
문제가 많은 집들
제마다 불운

However finally BH(blue house)
Only shaking the nation
Usually it's ruling power and
Some of those who followers
Every them have a problem

결국 청와대
국가를 뒤흔드는
집권 세력과
이를 따르는 자들
다 문제 있다

Waterloo 워터루(ABBA 히트곡)

What a beautiful team actually   아름다운 팀

Anytime they're right and proud   바르고 당당하고

Theirs singing power is good   가창력 좋아

Every time It's so great to me   너무 좋아요

Release any song by them   무슨 노랠 불러도

Listening sounds good to me   좋게만 들려

Of course I've heard many times   아무리 들어 봐도

Only it's the best so I love ABBA   요런 팀 없어

* ABBA

Year is go 세월이 간다
- Joe Biden -

Years opening now as new

새로운 세상

Especially Rodin think about it

로댕은 생각한다

A little bit skill and lot of luck

운 칠에 기 삼

Really about 80 years old now

미수米壽를 맞아

In this time leading the nation

국가를 지도하는

States leader's real image

지도자 모습

Go through a big challenge

도전을 헤쳐나갈

Oserbe the his leadership

자세를 본다

Available 이용 가용한, 유용한

Always peace is life   평화는 생명

Variety of harmony with trust   화합과 신뢰 속에

At the road to unification   통일로 가는

It's time to big turning point   일대 전환기에서

Large step is as bad as small step   과유는 불급

At once single step forward   한걸음씩 내딛고

Beside with America   미국과 함께

Long run keep the spirit alliance   동맹 정신 지키되

Every time avoid overconfidence   맹신은 금물

Blueberry 블루베리

Bluish berry

Like as ruby colored fruits

Usually come up best friend

Especially real present for me

Because of you are here

Even nature more beautiful

Really it is my pleasant and

Really just great the taste

You know filled with romance

블루 빛깔 띤

루비 머금은 과일

베스트 친구

리얼한 최고 선물

그대 있음에

대자연이 더 곱고

내게 기쁨 준

사근사근한 그 맛

랑만 넘치네

Butterfly 나비

But you would not come here	오지 못할 님
Usually I'd like to see you	늘 보고 싶은 그대
Today also I'm flying	**나**는 오늘도
Time to flying slowly	**늘**적거리며 난다
Everyday becomes butterfly	**한** 마리 나비
Really enchanted with magic	**마**법에 홀렸을까
Fantastic real imagination	**리**얼한 상상
Let's spread the wings	**나**래를 펼쳐 보자
Yellow flying wings	**비**상의 나래

Hard to say 쉽게 말 못해요

However the talk "I'm sorry"   미안하단 말

Actually I can't stop to say it, but   안 할 수도 없지만

Really I can't say to you   하진 못해요

Directly say that I love you   단지 사랑합니다

The story that can't be told   말 못할 사연

Of course I can't tell you quietly   은근히 못 밝혀도

So I'm stupid as you know   못난이라서

Always I can't explain it all   해명도 다 못하고

You know I feel so frustrated   요렇게 속만

Mountains 산

Maybe you say you leave me　　　가신다 하니

Often I feel sad without reason　　까닭 없이 서럽다

Usually I didn't cry with you　　운 적도 없고

Never had living with you too　　산 적도 없었지만

Talking toward you　　　　　　그대를 향해

Authentic open my mind　　　리얼한 가슴 열고

I confess to you sincerely　　고백을 한다

Now you think good relationship　인연을 생각해서

So you don't break connection　연락 끊지 마

Myself all 나 자신

Myself	나
You know increased something	는다
So regardless of time	무시로
Eventually out of rhythm	엇박자도
Lots of eerie mood	으스스하게
Finally dotage evenly	로망끼도
Actually began to it	사실상
Lots of growth	는 채
Last road be on the way	가

September 9월

She came here from hell

Early come around by cross wall

Perhaps she like a thief

Time to masking now

Every time I feel sick of it

Maybe the day so far go back

By the soothe and keep rules

Every day spending time anyway

Really no choice to other way

구천을 돌아

월담 해서 찾아온

도적 같은 놈

지금 마스크

나부터 지겹지만

갈 날은 멀다

달래가면서

이럭저럭 보낸다

다른 수 없다

Zacchaeus 삭개오(성경에 나오는 인물)

Zipped memory don't forget

Alive at the edge of the tongue

Certainly a true shout

Certainly so hotly

However exchanged tongues

Adorable lady and gentleman

Ecstatic scene of lovers

Usually after for a time

So it'll become withered

잊지 못하지

혀 끝에 살아 있는

진실된 외침

그토록 화끈하게

설왕 설래 한

레이디와 젠틀맨

임이라 황홀

잠시 시간 흐르면

시들해 진다

10 Line Poem
10 행시

Corona blue 코로나 우울증

Corona situation is on going
Often I walk on the road and
Raise or walking a local hill
Only live a roman nowadays
New relationship of human is
At once wrong it break down

Business call comes in I'll go
Literary society if there's I'll go
Usually I can't eat without it
Every time eat all the food well

코로나에도
로드 워킹과
나 홀로 산행하고
로망 다지며 산다

인간 관계는
한번 가면 끝

불러주면 나가고
안 불러도 나간다

없어 못 먹지
다 잘 먹는다

Jesus Cross 예수님 십자가

Jesus bless you	주여 비오니
Every way light up please	가는 길 밝히시고
So as far away as possible	가급적 멀리
Usually divine holy spirit	신령한 성령으로
Surely open the right way	길 터 주소서
Cross of under there	십자가 아래
Really look at myself	자신을 돌아보며
Only poor spirit and	가난한 심령
Support with righteously	의롭게 도우도록
Surely open right way	길 터 주소서

Stay with me   내 곁에 머물러 주세요

Stand with me please

Take not you leave here

Add energy to me

You know I'm satisfied

내 옆에 서서

곁을 떠나지 마오

에너지 보태 주니

만족합니다

While you stay here

I love you surely

Talk to you "I love you"

Hot so much like this

머무는 동안

물론 사랑합니다

러브 유 올웨이스

요래 뜨겁게

May diligently writing

Everyday without dissipate

부지런히 글 쓰는

디스 없는 일상사

Summer wine 섬머 와인

She came to see me   그녀가 왔다
Unusual something as pale condition   해쓱한 모습
Maybe she got a hurt till now   여태 입은 상처로
Missed gallant at all   름름함 다 잃었다
Even that guy who throw out her   내친 그 놈을
Refused talk to me about who is he   내색 않지만

Want to make clear and then   찜찜함 밝혀
I try take to him a hot compress but   찜통에 넣고픈데
Nobody is here do that to her   했다는 놈이 없다
Everyone don't know also exactly   다 모른단다

Three Seven 쓰리 세븐

Today get up early   일찍 일어나

However I'm writing it   이글을 쓴다

Really a fresh idea   삼빡한 생각

Every day by day disappear   사라져 가고

Even only nowadays   오로지 지금

So just have a sixth sense   육감만 갖고

Even though go the ground   칠떡 대지만

Very live and alive   팔팔 살아서

Every months keep grumbling   구시렁 대며

Now December has come   십이월 맞네

While alive   살아 있는 동안

When I was living in Gangnam	강남 살면서
However I went to Euljiro a lot	을지로 자주 나가
In there across the street	건너편 골목
Large room in the garret	너른 다락방에서
Every night wear cotton T-shirt	면 티만 입고

Anyway enjoy hugging with her	안고 뒹굴고
Long time stayed if possible	되는 날은 늦도록
I spending time slowly	는실대면서
Variously be together with her	이것 저것 다 나눈
Especially unusual relationship	유별난 그대

Astrazeneka 아스트라제네카 백신

All right it's too late

Start is hurry now

Therefore if catch in a ankle

Ruin on the live state

Anyway if can't buy on time

Zero is almost your fate

Eventually we've no card

Now get a shot or not

Everyone pain or not

Key complaint comes out

Actually have all the reason

아차 늦었다

스타트가 급하다

트집 잡히면

라이브로 망칠라

제 때 못 사면

네 운명도 끝이다

카드도 없다

맞든 말든 알아서

아프든 말든

볼멘 소리 나오는

까닭이 있지

Corona virus 코로나 바이러스

Could be they are zombie

Or troublemaking against all

Right away going out and then

Only you must corona test

Now if you hide further like it

Actually masks become useless

좀비가 되어

나라 어지럽히며

댕기지 말고

기어나와 검사 해

지금 숨으면

마스크도 헛 거야

Very high stubborn with you

If widespread toward out side

Right away infect more

Unbelievable if you get infect

So you may die

고집이 세서

집 밖에 노출되면

접족만 늘고

어쩌다 감염되면

요단강 간다

Interesting 흥미로운, 재미있는, 놀라운

If you interesting about it?	그것에 관심 있어?
Nowadays you still do that...	그게 여전히 좋아?
That is a love...	그것은 사랑이야
Every day you talk with them	그들과 대화하고
Recieve or reply that from them	그 말을 들어주고
Even if that's a small or useless	그것이 사소해도
Sustain do that	그걸 지속 하세요
That is a love	그건 사랑이니까
I'm full interesting about it	그것에 빠졌어요
Nobody do that very well but	그걸 잘은 못해도
Go ahead then you can suceed	그래야 성공해요

It was Friday 금요일이었어

It's finished in a verse 1 anyway
There is good to be simple

일절로 끝나니까
단출해서 좋아요

Write short just three line
All contained even difficult words
So let's open it up at will

짤막한 석줄 글에
막말 쉰말 다 담고
한바탕 펼쳐 봐요

Friday is lucky day to writers
Really enough poetic sentiment
It's endless even if you do more
Day by day leave many nice writing
Actually before you leave here
You'd better publish a poetry book

행운의 금요일엔
시심이 넘쳐나서
가도가도 끝없고

좋은 글 많이 남겨
아직 관 짜기 전에
요런 시집 내봐요

Times a while 잠시

There is own small routine 소소한 일상

It's avoid serious illness well 중병 잘도 피하고

Maybe it's been a long time 한참 흘렀다

Even though time is passed 시간은 지났어도

So it's not simple situations 간단치 않아

Always corona rot in me anyway 속 썩히는 코로나

Well disinfecting is better now 소독 잘 하고

However attend major meeting 중요 모임만 가되

If you go out side and stay long 한 데 나가면

Let's wash hands more actually 추가로 손 씻는 게

Every time it's very important 역수로 중요

Today's pains 오늘의 고통(은 내일의 향기다)

Terrible lover who no return
Of course I'm waiting all the time
Disperse of injury
At the extreme of pains
Yeah, I feel sad behind the scenes
Stare at tomorrow

Perhaps the lapse of time is big but
At times I have a doubt
If I would be burning incense
Next I would be praying true heart
See him again?

오지 않는 님
늘 기다린다

고별 후유증
통증이 도질 때면
은연중 섧다

내일을 향한
일구월심 크지만
의심도 든다

향불 피우고
기원 정성 들이면
다시 볼까나?

Acrostic 행시行詩(line poem)

Actually	참
Be good	좋은
Could metaphorically	은유로
Definitely fill me up	나를 채울
Even though stately friend	의젓한 친구
Friend of the friend	벗 중에 벗이여
Get along if with you	그대와 함께 하면
However more funny world	이 세상 더욱 즐겁고
I'm feeling be proud	름름해 지는 느낌이오
Just learn a lesson in a hush	은연중에 교훈도 얻으니
Know it life flows into poem	행시 속으로 인생이 흐르고
Lot rewarding by good start	시작이 좋아서 보람 또한 크다

Autumn leaves 단풍잎

Actually my age is..
Under the late fall in my life
Thinking about on the past
Usually I'd accelerated and
Make another exciting event
Now and than that was erotic

Leaves lose beautiful colors
Emaciated my face nowadays
And lose weight of the body
Valuable living changed other
Every day by day to the poor
So scratched looks like now

내 나이 벌써
인생 만추를 맞아
생각해 보면

가속하면서
을밋함 잊은 그땐
에로틱했지

단물 빠지고
풍광 초췌해 지니
잎사귀 말라

붉은 기운도
을씨년스레 변해
까칠해 지네

Winter season 겨울철

What a snow flower
Ice snow doesn't any smell
Now snow falls beautifully

There is nice purple sky
Every time make fine powder
Right now we've having a party

So during the winter living
Even in a gloomy heart
Actually I stumble

So my empty afternoon
Only with real longing
Now I'm look up to that

눈꽃 그대는
꽃내도 안 풍기고
이쁘게 내려

보라 빛 하늘
고운 가루 만들어
파티 벌이네

겨우살이로
울적해진 마음에
비척거리며

내 텅 빈 오후
리얼한 그리움에
고개 쳐든다

Winter season 겨울철

What a pretty mood 올망졸망한

It's a belief as a mustard seed 겨자씨 만한 믿음

Now ready to move 울먹거린다

There is own particular life 맞춤 인생에

Each couldn't achieve goals yet 아직 이루지 못한

Remained some feelings 서먹서먹함

Still I've dream to do what 일탈 꿈꾸며

Early started my step once 한번 내친 발걸음

Aloft hold up straight 번쩍 쳐든다

So tomorrow and tomorrow 내일 또 내일

Of course not much things to do 볼일 많지 않지만

Nowadays I calling nice magpie 까치부른다

13 Line Poem
13 행시

Because of fall 가을 때문일까

Beside autumn is passing

Even though dreary nowadays

Common sense of these days

All the time enjoy solutude

Usually I'm lonely old man alone

So all day long

Every day I'm lazy

On late autumn

Finally I've a strong line poem

Few fellow as clean

Always keeping with writers

Learn English line poems

Let's try hard now?

가을이 간다

을씨년스러워도

이런 때에는

고독 씹으며

독방 늙은이 되어

하루 왼종일

게으름 부려본다

만추라지만

든든한 행시 있어

때묻지 않은

문우들 교감하며

일단 영어행시나

까뒤집을까 ?

I need you Jesus 오 전능하신 하나님 나의 예수님

I need you Jesus also today	오늘도 예수님이 필요합니다
Now I can't live without you	**전** 당신 없이는 살 수 없어요
Every day God gives power	**능**력 주시는 하나님
Every day more and more	**하**루 하루 점점 더
Dear my lovely bridegroom	**신**랑되신 나의 사랑스러운 주님
You have ravished my heart	**하**나님은 나를 기쁘게 하십니다
Of course you are my thee	**나**의 하나님
Usually I need you	**님**이 늘 필요합니다
Jesus is my lovely bridegroom	**나**의 신랑 되신 예수님
Everyday depends on the Lord	**의**지합니다 매일 매일
So sweet to my taste	**예**수님은 제게 너무 달콤해요
Uniformly lots of days	**수**많은 날들 한결 같이
Sustain me with your love	**님**의 사랑으로 나를 지탱합니다

Green color you 초록빛 그대

Generally all winter below zero   겨울 영하에

Right now don't be so upset   울상 지을 일 없다

Every day with pride minded   의연한 자세

Edge of it take long sip   길게 한모금 빨고

Now wet my throat   목젖 축인다

Can you stand up there   딛고 선다면

Only it's top valuable land   고도 가치 있는 땅

Low pick to cross the top anyway   넘어야 할 산

Of course fate to meet actually   어차피 만날 운명

Right hug each other   서로 보듬고

You rather open your eyes   다소곳 뜬 눈

On these days start is green   시작부터 푸르다

Usually good to see you Spring   봄아 반갑다

October Forest 10월의 숲

On my optimistic life   낙관적 삶에

Colorful leaves become thick   엽색은 짙어가고

The autumn wind blows at times   이따금 추풍

Often troubled with others   더러는 부대끼고

Be while a heart of excitement   욱 하는 심정

Eventually swallows in folds   고이 접어 삼킨다

Really that also my destiny   운명이려니

Finally I have a little left   나머지 남은

Over the trace of righteous life   의로운 흔적 위로

Red my autumn is ripe   가을은 익고

Even poorly my day   을밋한 날도

Seeing at the round sky   동그란 하늘 보며

Take draw on my canvas   화폭 채운다

You Corona 코로나 너!

⇩

가라 **가**	**G**o! Go out!
안 나가**나**	**H**owever don't you go out?
눈치만 보**다**	**I**n these day just looking at it
영 주저 앉을**라**	**J**ust gonna sit down forever
비행기 티켓 주**마**	**K**orean Air ticket I'll give you
내가 진정 원하는 **바**	**L**et's talk what I really want
내 말 잘 들으면 넌 신**사**	**M**ay listen you're gentleman
가을 전 떠나는 게 좋**아**	**N**otice! You leave before fall
잘 하는지 지켜 보**자**	**O**nly I'll watch you about it
제대로 하는 절**차**	**P**roper procedure you do it
잘 되면 한잔 **카**	**Q**uiet if it works well I'll drink
잘 가라 스**타**	**R**eally goodbye to star
외치고 **파**	**S**o I wanna to shout
푸하**하**	**T**hen I'll smile ha ha ha

- 가나다라 #217

/ 2021.3.7 -

116

Don't forget poem   시를 잊지 마세요

Did you have been go there?   가 봤어 거기?

Of course I've been there many   나는 여러 번 갔지

Nowadays lots of persons visit   다들 오던데

Take the last time?   라스트로 오려나?

Forecast says good weather   마침 날씨도

Or even wind conditions nice   바람 적당한 때라

Really you come steal in   사알짝 와 봐

Going on little bit earlier but   아직 일러도

Ensemble leaves as prepared   자리잡은 꽃잎들

Times pass more and more   차차 열리면

Perhaps by word of mouth   카더라 통신 타고

Only spread out everywhere   타지에 퍼져

Every times visit cloud waves   파도처럼 올 거야

Maybe around white season   하얀 봄날에

– 가나다라 #205

/ 2019.5.2 –

Korean language 한글

Know the Korean language and 한글을 알고
Of course write English line poem 글로 행시를 쓴다
Really I'm happy day by day 날로 기쁘다
Each letters are own language so 우리 글이라
Amazing pride makes me excited 리얼한 자긍심에
Now these articles pretty shine 글이 빛난다

Language meaning is happiness 행복의 의미
Always achieve it anyway 시인이 일궈내고
Noble work get recognized 인정 받으며
Generally leading it quietly 은근히 앞장 선다
Usually live with line poems 행시에 묻혀 사는
All the time day and day 복된 나날이
Good as much as great 하늘 만큼 땅 만큼
Every time is all beautiful 다 아름답다

Pretty Blue Eyes 아름다운 푸른 눈동자

Pretty of you now	그대는 지금
Really curious where are you from	대체 어디서 왔나
Eyes so clear always	맑은 눈동자
Thou are so beautiful quietly	은은한 자태
The moment of eye contact	눈이 마주친 순간
You know the energy rises	에너지 불끈
But without the reason	나도 모르게
Looking and keep going into you	자꾸만 빨려 들고
Usually feeling of excitement	신명 나는 느낌과
Energy is good caused by you	이 좋은 기분
Eyes closed for a moment	잠시 눈 감고
You know I try to calm down	겨우 진정해 보지만
Eventually in the presence of you	든직한 그 모습에
So open my eyes again	다시 눈 뜬다

15 Line Poem
15 행시

English line poem 영어 행시

Everyday I'm writing in English	영어로 쓴다
No major in language studies	어학 전공 안 해도
Go to roma in line poem cafe	로마에 와서
Learn write and read like this	쓰고 읽고 배우며
I spend many times in this way	는적거리니
So ready to line poem shaped	행시 모양 갖추고
However it rise poetic mind	시심 솟는다
Lead Han-haeng literary society	한행문학 이끌며
I gather the writing comrade	글 동지 모아
Now write with roman sentence	로망 담긴 글 쓰는
Everyday we meet proud of it	도도한 나날
Play together nice fellow writer	멋진 문우 함께 한
Of course it's true friendship	진정한 우정
Ever development of line poem	행시 문학 발전의
Make dig a real touchstone	시금석 캔다

120

Love Your Destiny 네 운명을 사랑하라
- Amor Fati -

Let me ask you	네게 물어 보고파
Often if we are lucky	운이 좋으면
Very wonder be long-lived	명도 길어지는지
Estimate inaccurate formula	을밋한 공식
Yesterday I love someone	사랑하는 사람과
On rendezvous days	랑데부 할 때
Usually have been all day	하루 종일 붙어서
Radio listening and	라디오 듣고
Day by day without fault	니캉 허물도 없이
Every time with face folded	체면도 접고
So I was closer with you	가까워졌던 거지
There was a good time	한참 좋다가
I made a mistake once	말 한번 잘못 해서
Next time she left and then	이별 하더니
You know I'm still separated	지금껏 남남이네

121

National Cemetery 국립묘지

Now I'm seventy years old	나이는 칠순
All day go past very very fast	는적댈 새도 없다
Tired accumulated much more	누적된 피로
If it's fast then before too late	가속도 붙기 전에
Of course I will try something	뭐든 할 거야
No arrived the last time	라스트 찍기 전에
Anyway I will do something	해 보고 싶고
Let me try to challenge	도전하고자 한다
Call all our line poet	대한민국 행시인
Especially focused it here only	한 곳에 집중
Means zoomsi with national pride	민족혼 주먹행시
Extent to whole Korean national	국민에 확산
The day when approved official	공식 인정 받는 날
Especially take certification shot	인증 샷 찍고
Really appear successor for me	이을 사람 생기면
You know I will handover him all	다 물려 준다

The end of the month 그믐날

Today is 31 May 오늘은 5.31
However everything goes by turn 늘 돌고 도는 세상
Enjoy each time implicitly 은근 즐겁다

Especially the May already gone 오월은 이미
Now get over the wall 월담 하고 사라져
Day over naturally 의례 끝났지

Of course the end means start 끝은 또 시작
Finally coming a new day 날은 다시 와

Take care every business but 조심도 하고
However often shows courage 용기 있게 살면서
Every moment I will success 히트 칠 거야

My opinion is up to the last 마지막까지
Of course avoid impossibility 무리수 삼가면서
No risk personal relations 리스크 없는
Therefore live my whole life 한평생 보내기로
Honorable dreams again 다시 꿈꾼다

The last chance 마지막 기회다

Always have to burning yourself	태워야 한다
But you don't listen funny	우습게 듣지 말고
Can you wake up now?	지금 일어나?
Day by day think the challenge	도전을 생각하라
Every time you can do it	못할 게 뭐냐
Finally you do if you can	할 수 있으면 한다
Good chance is right now	지금이 기회
However with unique presence	독보적 존재감에
I do if you do it too	한다면 한다
Just find a way to do it	가능한 방법 찾아
Kill the time anyway	슴벅대면서
Let on trust gentle and stickness	은근과 끈기 믿고
Must overcome you would	이뤄내야 해
Now if you going to give up	제때 포기할 생각
Only you'd better fold that idea	묻어 두고서
Please get it whatever you do	어떻게든 잡아라
Quickly take the last chance	라스트 찬스

The world is not easy -
세상은 절대로만만 하지 않아요

The world is not easy
However more than imagine
Every moment difficult in a hush

Whatever nothing is easy
Often we dream of big hit
Right now lottery winning is
Lot easier than we thought
Definitely it's not easy

If you go through the world
Surely going to be now?

No, I don't think so
Our lives in the past
There is like unknown world

Except the clear side
And other side we didn't seen
So many of it in the world
You think was it easy to fluke?

세상은 쉽지 않아
상상 그 이상으로
은근히 어렵지요

절대 쉬운 건 없어
대박 꿈 꿔 보지만
로또 복권 당첨이
만만할 것 같아도
만만치 않습니다

하물며 세상 일이
지금처럼 쉽나요?

않다고 생각해요
아직까지 살면서
요지경 같은 세상

해맑은 면 외에도
보지 못한 구석이
세상 속에 많아요
요행이 쉽던가요?

행시야 놀자 ^{시리즈} **11**

쉬운영어행시

2021년 4월 30일 발행

저　　자　정 동 희
이 메 일　daumsaedai@hanmail.net

인쇄·유통　영상복음
편　　집　정 동 희
발　　행　도서출판 한행문학
등　　록　관악바 00017 (2010.5.25)
주　　소　서울시 중구 을지로 18길 12
전　　화　02-730-7673 / 010-6309-2050
팩　　스　02-730-7675
카　　페　http://cafe.daum.net/3LinePoem
홈페이지　www.hangsee.com

정　　가　**6,000원**
I S B N　978-89-97952-41-0-04810
　　　　　978-89-97952-40-3-04810(세트번호)

공급처 ┃ 가나북스 www.gnbooks.co.kr
전　화 ┃ 031-959-8833(代)
전　화 ┃ 031-959-8834